# Cool

# REFASHIONED T-SHIRTS

FUN & EASY FASHION PROJECTS

ALEX KUSKOWSKI

**Checkerboard Library**

An Imprint of Abdo Publishing
abdopublishing.com

**abdopublishing.com**

Published by Abdo Publishing, a division of ABDO, PO Box 398166, Minneapolis, Minnesota 55439. Copyright © 2016 by Abdo Consulting Group, Inc. International copyrights reserved in all countries. No part of this book may be reproduced in any form without written permission from the publisher. Checkerboard Library™ is a trademark and logo of Abdo Publishing.

Printed in the United States of America, North Mankato, Minnesota

062015
092015

Design and Production: Jen Schoeller, Mighty Media, Inc.
Series Editor: Liz Salzmann
Photo Credits: Jen Schoeller, Shutterstock

The following manufacturers/names appearing in this book are trademarks: Tulip®, Mod Podge®

**Library of Congress Cataloging-in-Publication Data**

Kuskowski, Alex, author.
Cool refashioned t-shirts : fun & easy fashion projects / Alex Kuskowski.
    pages cm. -- (Cool refashion)

Audience: Grades 4 to 6.
Includes index.
ISBN 978-1-62403-705-4

1. T-shirts--Juvenile literature. 2. Dress accessories--Juvenile literature. 3. Fashion design--Juvenile literature. 4. Handicraft for girls--Juvenile literature. I. Title.

TT675.K87 2016
646.4--dc23
                      2014045323

## To Adult Helpers

This is your chance to assist a new crafter! As children learn to craft, they develop new skills, gain confidence, and make cool things. These activities are designed to help children learn how to make their own craft projects. They may need more assistance for some activities than others. Be there to offer guidance when they need it. Encourage them to do as much as they can on their own. Be a cheerleader for their creativity.

Before getting started, remember to lay down ground rules for using tools and supplies and for cleaning up. There should always be adult supervision when using a sharp tool.

# Table of Contents

# RESTART YOUR WARDROBE

## Shape UP Your Shirts

Get started refashioning! Refashioning is all about reusing things you already have. You can turn them into new things that you'll love.

Take your T-shirts from **drab** to fab. You can use T-shirts to make headbands, bags, or necklaces.

## Permission & Safety

- Always get **permission** before making crafts at home.

- Ask whether you can use the tools and materials needed.

- Ask for help if you need it.

- Be careful with sharp and hot objects such as knives and irons.

## Be Prepared

- Read the entire activity before you begin.

- Make sure you have everything you need to do the project.

- Follow directions carefully.

- Clean up after you are finished.

Basic terms and step-by-step instructions will make redoing your closet a breeze. These projects will help you turn T-shirts into one-of-a-kind fashion pieces.

# DOWN TO a T

T-shirts are one of the most **versatile** clothes to refashion! You can remake a T-shirt into almost anything. All it takes is a little **imagination.**

## WORKING WITH SHIRTS

IF POSSIBLE, USE FABRIC SCISSORS. THEY ARE MADE FOR CUTTING FABRIC.

WASH ALL SHIRTS BEFORE YOU USE THEM IN CRAFT PROJECTS.

DRAW WHERE YOU WILL CUT WITH CHALK FIRST TO AVOID MAKING MISTAKES.

# Refashion Ideas for T-shirts

## SUPER SCISSORS

- Cut up old clothing. Reuse the fabric for a new fashion project.
- Trim off the sleeves or collar of a T-shirt for a new look!
- Cut the back of a T-shirt in a cool shape! Try a heart or triangle.

## COLOR CHANGE

- Dye light-colored clothing any color of the rainbow.
- Bleach dark clothes to bring in new color.

## ADD SPARKLE

- Glue on gems with fabric glue.
- Add beads to clothing with thread and a needle.

## RIBBON RUN

- Attach ribbons to an old T-shirt in a pretty pattern.
- Glue lace on old clothes for a twist.

# TOOLS & MATERIALS

CARDBOARD

CASSETTE TAPE

FABRIC PAINT

FLIP-FLOPS

FOAM BRUSH

GRAPHIC T-SHIRT

HOT GLUE GUN
& GLUE STICKS

IRON

IRON-ON FUSING WEB

LACY TABLECLOTH
OR SCARF

MEASURING TAPE

MOD PODGE

# HERE ARE SOME OF THE THINGS YOU'LL NEED FOR THE PROJECTS IN THIS BOOK.

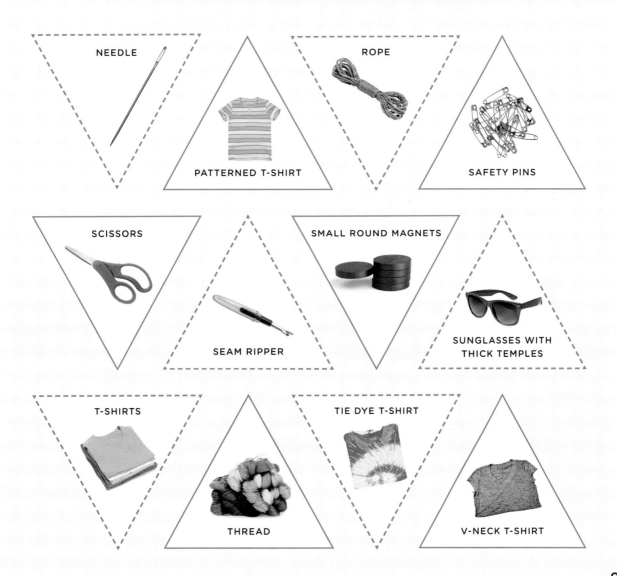

NEEDLE

PATTERNED T-SHIRT

ROPE

SAFETY PINS

SCISSORS

SEAM RIPPER

SMALL ROUND MAGNETS

SUNGLASSES WITH THICK TEMPLES

T-SHIRTS

THREAD

TIE DYE T-SHIRT

V-NECK T-SHIRT

# PERFECT
## FIT BOW

Try this Headband on for Size!

1. Cut four rectangles out of the T-shirt. Make them the following sizes.

> 2 by 21 inches (5 by 56 cm)
> 2 by 4 inches (5 by 10 cm)
> 2 by 4 inches (5 by 10 cm)
> 1 by 4 inches (2.5 by 10 cm)

2. Fold one short side of the largest rectangle over. Lay a piece of fusing web along the edge. Iron it following the instructions on the package. Remove the backing. Fold the opposite side over so that it covers the fusing web. Iron it in place.

3. Iron a piece of fusing web to one side of the smallest rectangle. Remove the backing.

4. Put the two matching rectangles on top of each other. Lay them **lengthwise** over the seam of the headband. Pinch the fabric together. Wrap the small rectangle around the fabric. Iron it to seal it in place.

11

# T-SHIRT
# FLiP-FLOPS

Take Your Flip-Flops up a Notch!

## WHAT YOU NEED

T-SHIRT
MEASURING TAPE
SCISSORS
FLIP-FLOPS
HOT GLUE GUN &
GLUE STICKS

1. Cut the shirt **horizontally** into strips. Make them 1 inch (2.5 cm) wide. The strips will have two layers.

2. Glue the end of a strip to the **thong** of a flip-flop. Wrap the strip around one of the straps. Stretch the strip as you wrap it. Cover the strap. Hot glue the end of the strip to the back of the strap.

3. Wrap the other strap with a second T-shirt strip.

4. Repeat steps 2 and 3 with the other flip-flop.

5. Glue strips to the back of the straps to make **gladiator sandals**.

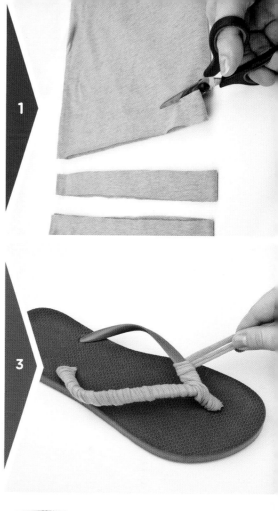

13

# GRAB 'N' GO BAG

## Make a Cute Travel Tote!

**WHAT YOU NEED**

GRAPHIC T-SHIRT

SCISSORS

MEASURING TAPE

1. Lay the shirt flat. Cut off the bottom hem. Cut off the sleeves along the seams.

2. Fold the shirt in half **lengthwise**. Cut from the folded side up to the shoulder. Mirror the curve of the armholes.

3. Unfold the shirt. Make vertical cuts in the bottom of the shirt. Make the cuts 6 inches (15 cm) long and 1 inch (2.5 cm) wide.

4. Pull on the ends of the strips to stretch them out.

5. Match the strips from opposite sides of the shirt together. Tie each pair of strips together in a knot.

# BOLD 'N' BEAUTIFUL Sunglasses

## Shine as Bright as the Sun!

16

1. Cut two rectangles out of the T-shirt. Make them 6 by 2 inches (15 by 5 cm).

2. Brush a thin layer of Mod Podge on the outside of a **temple**.

3. Carefully smooth one of the rectangles over Mod Podge. Let it dry.

4. Trim the fabric ¼ inch (.5 cm) around the temple. Make a few cuts in the fabric along the curve of the temple.

5. Brush Mod Podge on the inside of the temple. Press the fabric over the Mod Podge. Let it dry.

6. Repeat steps 2 through 5 to cover the other temple.

*Cover other items with old shirts. Try a glasses case, **wallet**, or journal!*

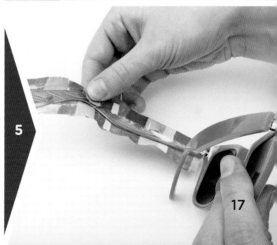

# LACE IT UP
## *Tee*

### Make It Fashion Forward!

**WHAT YOU NEED**

LACY TABLECLOTH OR SCARF

SCISSORS

SEAM RIPPER

V-NECK T-SHIRT

NEEDLE

THREAD

MEASURING TAPE

1. Cut off the corner of the tablecloth or **scarf**. Use a seam ripper to carefully remove the lace from the cloth.

2. Lay the lace on the shirt. Line the edge of the lace up with the edge of the neckline.

3. Thread the needle. Tie a knot at one end of the thread.

4. Push the needle up through the shirt and the lace near the edge of the neckline. Move the needle about ¼ inch (.5 cm) along the neckline. Push the needle down through the lace and the shirt.

5. Repeat step 4 until the lace is sewn to the shirt. Knot the thread on the inside of the shirt.

*Even Cooler!*

*Try using ribbon instead of lace!*

# maGNetic
## PULL BRACELET

*You Can't Resist Them!*

1. Cut two strips of fabric from each shirt. Make them 1 inch (2.5 cm) wide and as long as the shirts. Cut out two rectangles. Make them 3 by 1 inches (7.5 by 2.5 cm).

2. Hot glue one end of each of the strips together. Separate the strips into three groups of two.

3. Braid the strips together. Stop when the braid can wrap around your wrist twice. Cut the strips. Hot glue the ends together.

4. Wrap one rectangle around one end of the braid. Hot glue it in place. Wrap the other end of the braid with the other rectangle the same way. Trim off the extra material.

5. Hot glue a magnet to one end of the braid. Let it dry. Stick the second magnet to the glued magnet. Hot glue the other end of the braid to the second magnet. Let it dry. Separate the magnets and wind the braid around your wrist twice to wear it.

# CORDED
## NECKLACE

**WHAT YOU NEED**

TIE-DYED T-SHIRT
SCISSORS
MEASURING TAPE
HOT GLUE GUN &
GLUE STICKS

1. Cut off the bottom hem of the T-shirt. Cut across the shirt under the sleeves.

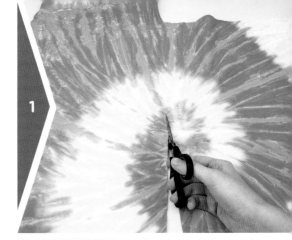

2. Cut the bottom of the shirt into 1-inch (2.5 cm) strips. Cut across the shirt to make large loops.

3. Cut a rectangle out of the top of the shirt. Make it 3 inches (7 cm) by 6 inches (14 cm).

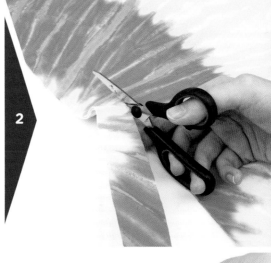

4. Hold the loops together. Wrap the rectangle around the loops. Hot glue the end of the rectangle in place. Let it dry.

*Even Cooler!*

*Cut strips from several shirts to add more color!*

23

# PLAY-IT-AGAIN
## Tee

**WHAT YOU NEED**

CARDBOARD

T-SHIRT

3 CASSETTE TAPES

FABRIC PAINT,
3 COLORS

FOAM BRUSH

### Show Your Love of Jams on Your Tee!

1 Put the cardboard inside the shirt.

2 Paint one side of a cassette tape with fabric paint. Press the cassette on the upper left side of the shirt.

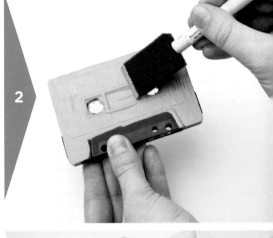

3 Stamp the cassette twice more under the first stamp. Paint the cassette before each stamp.

4 Make two more rows of cassette stamps using the other colors. Let the paint dry.

**Even Cooler!**

*Make your own stamp. Cut a sponge into any shape you want!*

# ROPED-UP Backpack

## Tie up with a Cool Backpack!

1. Cut a rectangle out of the shirt. Make it 18 by 24 inches (46 by 61 cm). Fold the rectangle in half **crosswise**.

2. Thread the needle with 30 inches (76 cm) of thread. Tie a knot at one end of the thread.

3. Sew the edges opposite the fold together. Stick the needle up through both layers of fabric. Bring the needle back under the fabric. Stick it up through the fabric again.

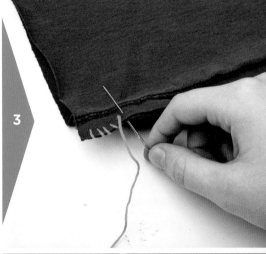

4. Repeat until you reach the end of the fabric. Knot the thread near the fabric. Cut off the extra thread.

5. Refold the rectangle with the sewn edge in the center. Sew one short edge of the rectangle together.

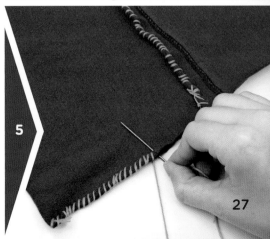

CONTINUED ON NEXT PAGE

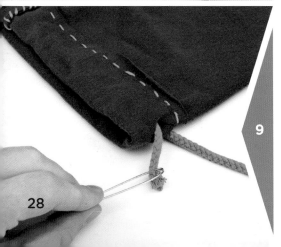

**6** Cut a slit on each side of the open edge of the bag along the fold.

**7** Fold the open edge down 2 inches (5 cm) all the way around. Sew along the edge of the fold. When you reach the end, knot the thread near the fabric. Cut off the extra thread.

**8** Cut two pieces of rope 110 inches (280 cm) long.

**9** Put a safety pin on one end of a rope. Push the pin through one of the slits. Use it to work the rope through the fold all the way around the bag. Pull the rope out through the same hole it entered.

**10** Repeat step 9 to thread the other rope through the other slit.

**11** Cut a small hole through both layers of fabric near each bottom corner.

**12** Bring the ends of the rope from the left slit together. Push them through the hole in the bottom left corner.

**13** Tie the ends of the rope into a knot.

**14** Repeat steps 12 and 13 with the rope from the right slit.

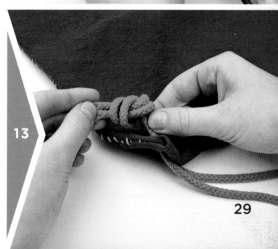

# CONCLUSION

Congratulations! You just refashioned some old T-shirts. But don't stop here! Take what you've learned to the next step. Try out your own ideas for reusing T-shirts. Make something **unique** and totally you!

Check out the other books in this series. Learn how to refashion jeans, **scarves**, sweaters, and more.

Get crafting today!

# GLOSSARY

**CROSSWISE –** in the direction of the shortest side.

**DRAB –** dull, plain, or uninteresting.

**GLADIATOR –** an ancient Roman fighter.

**HORIZONTALLY –** in the same direction as the ground, or side-to-side.

**IMAGINATION –** the creative ability to think up new ideas and form mental images of things that aren't real or present.

**LENGTHWISE –** in the direction of the longest side.

**PERMISSION –** when a person in charge says it's okay to do something.

**SANDAL –** a kind of shoe that is held on with straps.

**SCARF –** a long piece of cloth worn around the neck for decoration or to keep warm.

**TEMPLE –** one of the side parts of a pair of glasses that rest on the ears.

**THONG –** a sandal strap that goes between the toes.

**UNIQUE –** different, unusual, or special.

**VERSATILE –** having many uses.

**WALLET –** a flat case to keep money or pictures in.

# Websites

To learn more about Cool Refashion, visit **booklinks.abdopublishing.com**. These links are routinely monitored and updated to provide the most current information available.

# iNDeX